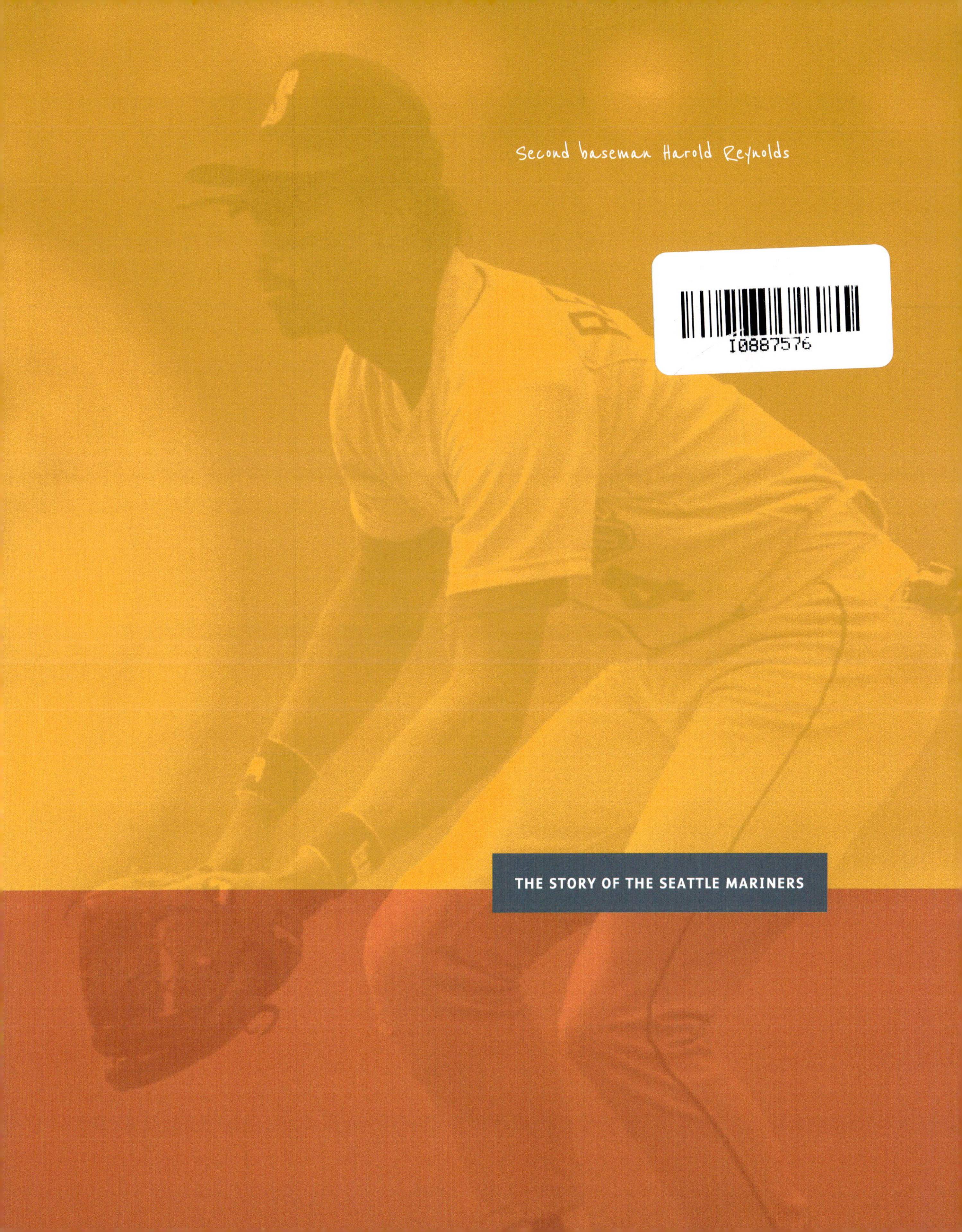

Second baseman Harold Reynolds

THE STORY OF THE SEATTLE MARINERS

Catcher Cal Raleigh

THE STORY OF THE

SEATTLE MARINERS

JIM WHITING

Center fielder Ken Griffey Jr.

CREATIVE SPORTS

CREATIVE EDUCATION / CREATIVE PAPERBACKS

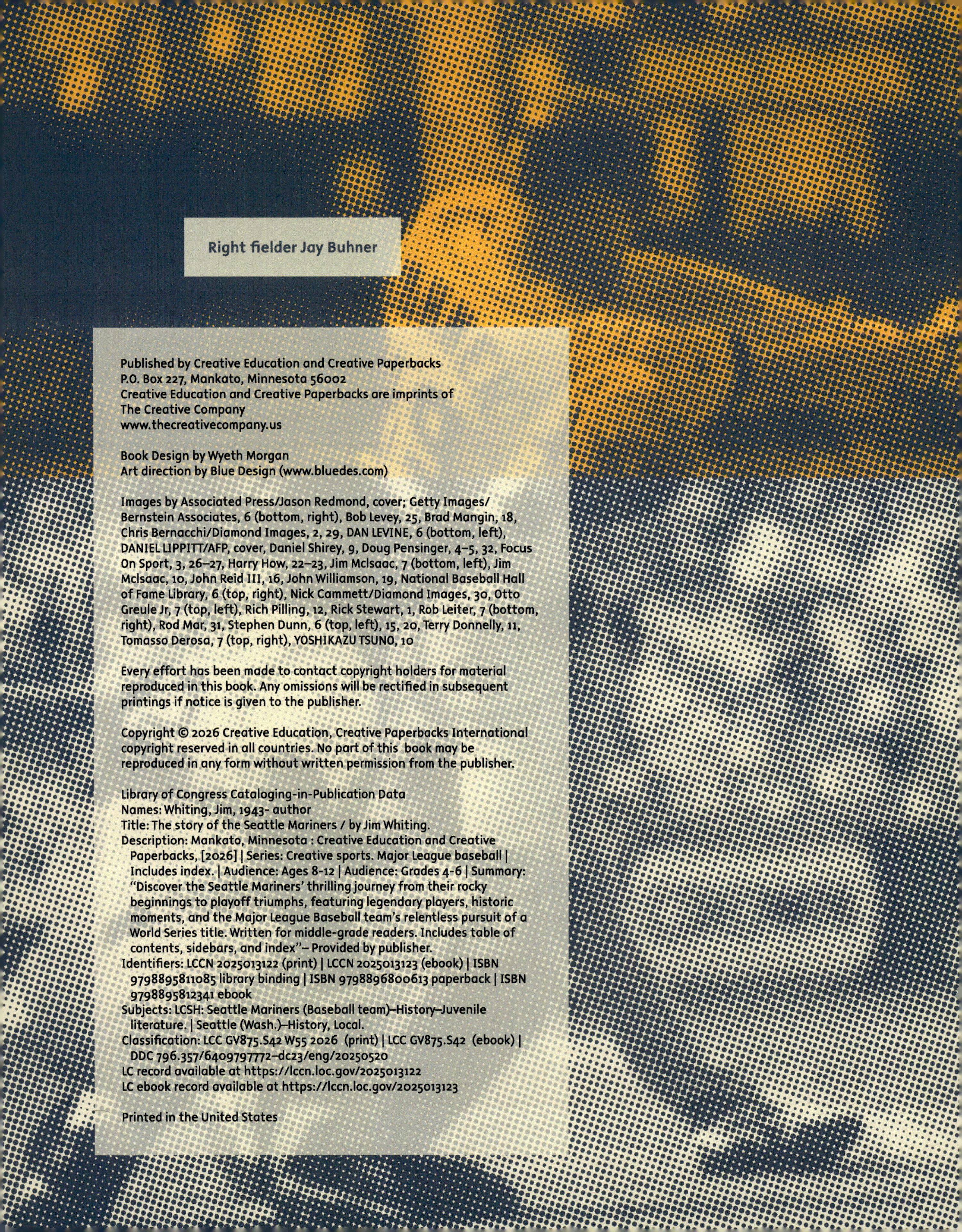

Right fielder Jay Buhner

Published by Creative Education and Creative Paperbacks
P.O. Box 227, Mankato, Minnesota 56002
Creative Education and Creative Paperbacks are imprints of
The Creative Company
www.thecreativecompany.us

Book Design by Wyeth Morgan
Art direction by Blue Design (www.bluedes.com)

Images by Associated Press/Jason Redmond, cover; Getty Images/ Bernstein Associates, 6 (bottom, right), Bob Levey, 25, Brad Mangin, 18, Chris Bernacchi/Diamond Images, 2, 29, DAN LEVINE, 6 (bottom, left), DANIEL LIPPITT/AFP, cover, Daniel Shirey, 9, Doug Pensinger, 4–5, 32, Focus On Sport, 3, 26–27, Harry How, 22–23, Jim McIsaac, 7 (bottom, left), Jim McIsaac, 10, John Reid III, 16, John Williamson, 19, National Baseball Hall of Fame Library, 6 (top, right), Nick Cammett/Diamond Images, 30, Otto Greule Jr, 7 (top, left), Rich Pilling, 12, Rick Stewart, 1, Rob Leiter, 7 (bottom, right), Rod Mar, 31, Stephen Dunn, 6 (top, left), 15, 20, Terry Donnelly, 11, Tomasso Derosa, 7 (top, right), YOSHIKAZU TSUNO, 10

Library of Congress Cataloging-in-Publication Data
Names: Whiting, Jim, 1943- author
Title: The story of the Seattle Mariners / by Jim Whiting.
Description: Mankato, Minnesota : Creative Education and Creative Paperbacks, [2026] | Series: Creative sports. Major League baseball | Includes index. | Audience: Ages 8-12 | Audience: Grades 4-6 | Summary: "Discover the Seattle Mariners' thrilling journey from their rocky beginnings to playoff triumphs, featuring legendary players, historic moments, and the Major League Baseball team's relentless pursuit of a World Series title. Written for middle-grade readers. Includes table of contents, sidebars, and index"– Provided by publisher.
Identifiers: LCCN 2025013122 (print) | LCCN 2025013123 (ebook) | ISBN 9798895811085 library binding | ISBN 9798896800613 paperback | ISBN 9798895812341 ebook
Subjects: LCSH: Seattle Mariners (Baseball team)–History–Juvenile literature. | Seattle (Wash.)–History, Local.
Classification: LCC GV875.S42 W55 2026 (print) | LCC GV875.S42 (ebook) | DDC 796.357/6409797772–dc23/eng/20250520
LC record available at https://lccn.loc.gov/2025013122
LC ebook record available at https://lccn.loc.gov/2025013123

Printed in the United States

MOSES
12
SASAKI
22

CONTENTS

EXTRA INNINGS

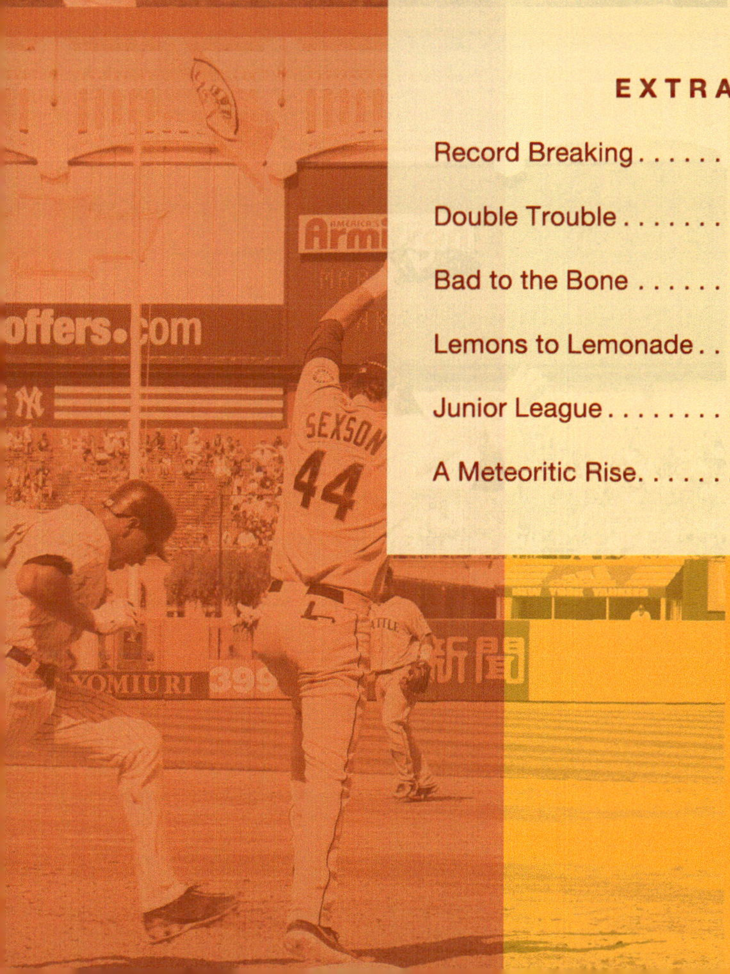

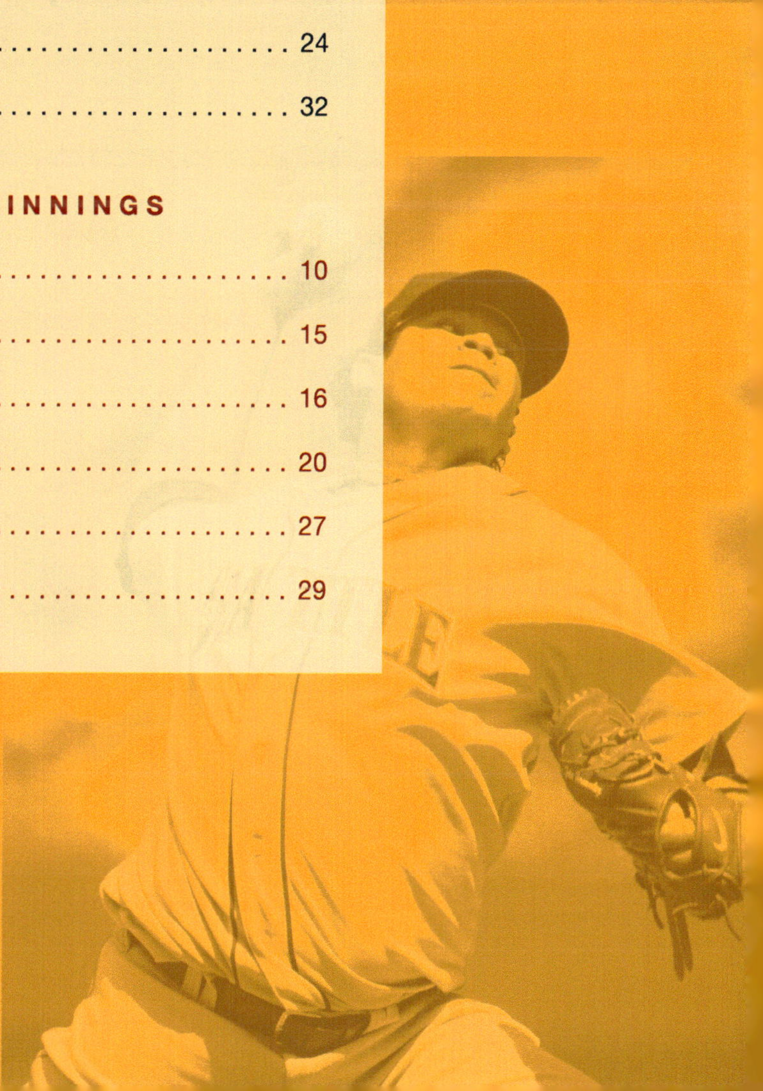

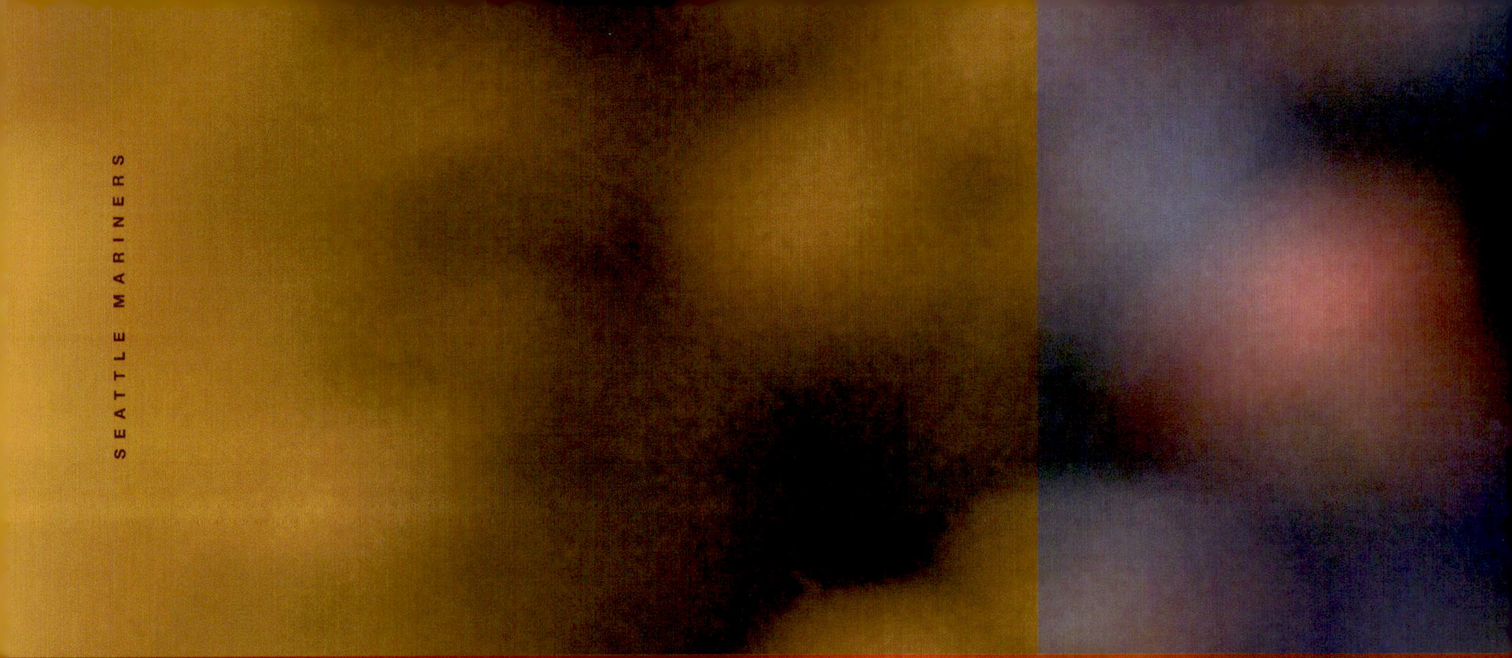

SCUTTLING THE POSTSEASON DROUGHT

Entering the 2022 Major League Baseball (MLB) season, the Seattle Mariners of the American League (AL) West Division had missed the postseason for 20 years in a row. That was the longest streak of futility of any major North American professional sport.

More than a third of the way through the season, there didn't seem to be much room for optimism for M's fans. The team had a record of 29 wins, 39 losses on June 19. Then they won eight of the next 10 games. That set the stage for a 14-game winning streak between July 2 and the All-Star break on July 17. It raised their record to 51–42.

Seattle continued to play good ball as the season wound down. On September 30, they were in contention for one of the three Wild Card slots in the playoffs. The Toronto Blue Jays were in the lead. Seattle was a game and a half behind. The Tampa Bay Rays trailed the Mariners by half a game. And the Baltimore Orioles were still in contention, five and a half games behind Seattle.

Second baseman Dylan Moore

EXTRA INNINGS

ICHIRO SUZUKI
OUTFIELDER
MARINERS SEASONS: 2001–2012, 2018
HEIGHT: 5-FOOT-11
WEIGHT: 175 POUNDS
KEY STATS: .311 BATTING AVERAGE, 117 HOME RUNS, 780 RBIS, 10X ALL-STAR

RECORD BREAKING

Ichiro Suzuki played the first nine years of his career with the Orix BlueWave of Nippon Professional Baseball. He joined the MLB in 2001 and quickly became a fan favorite with his smooth hitting, incredible speed, and strong defensive plays. Over his 14 seasons with the Mariners, Ichiro set numerous records, including an unforgettable season in 2004 when he broke the MLB record for most hits in a season with 262. His dedication and unique talent not only helped define an era for the Mariners but also left a lasting legacy. He is regarded as one of the greatest contact hitters, leadoff hitters, and defensive outfielders in baseball history.

Seattle skyline

As they took the field that night against the Oakland Athletics, the Mariners knew that a win would guarantee their spot in the playoffs, even if they lost all of next six games left to play. "Logically, there was no reason to be worried, but baseball is unpredictable and Seattle fans had been through far too much over the years to relax now," wrote Ben Blotner of the baseball research website sabr.org.

Seattle took a 1–0 lead in the first inning. Second baseman Dylan Moore led off with a single. He stole second. First baseman Ty France doubled him home. Oakland tied the score in the top of the second with a home run. Neither team could score after that.

The first two Seattle batters in the bottom of the ninth struck out. Seattle manager Scott Servais sent catcher Cal Raleigh to the plate as a pinch hitter. Raleigh had tied the Mariners record for home runs by a catcher with 25 in just his second year with the team. He worked the count to three balls and two strikes. Then he hit a long drive to right field. Would it land in fair territory? Yes!

Raleigh flipped his bat aside, skipped around the bases, and happily hopped onto home plate as his teammates mobbed him. Seattle won, 2–1. The long playoff drought was finally over!

Seattle
36

The celebration wasn't. Many fans stuck around to greet the members of the team as they emerged from the locker room an hour later and circled the perimeter of the field.

LAUNCHING THE MARINERS

The Mariners were not Seattle's first foray into the major leagues. The Seattle Pilots began play in 1969. Financial problems and stadium issues doomed the team. Its dismal 64–98 record did not help. The Pilots flew to Milwaukee, Wisconsin, before the next season. They became the Brewers.

The Mariners franchise was the result of an agreement between the city of Seattle and MLB to release the Pilots. The new team's name referred to the region's history of maritime trade. The Mariners played their first game on April 6, 1977. Fans packed the sold-out Kingdome. Seattle faced the Los Angeles Angels. The Angels won 7–0. It was the first of many Seattle defeats that season. The team finished 64–98. It was the same mark as the hapless Pilots.

Left fielder/first baseman Bruce Bochte joined the Mariners for their second season. He batted above .300 early in the season. "In the beginning, I was the only one hitting the ball," Bochte later recalled. "It got to the point that I felt if I didn't get two hits and drive in two runs, we wouldn't win the game." The pressure sent him into a prolonged slump. Seattle managed just 56 wins.

Things improved in 1979. The team went 67–95. The next two seasons were disappointments. Pitcher Floyd Bannister gave his best effort. But neither he nor Bochte could keep the club from backsliding. Veteran pitcher Gaylord Perry arrived in 1982. He brought 20 years' worth of experience to Seattle.

Pitcher Gaylord Perry

The "Ancient Mariner" celebrated his 300th career win that season. He helped boost the team to 76 wins.

In 1984, first baseman Alvin Davis was named Rookie of the Year. He finished the season with 27 home runs and 116 runs batted in (RBIs). Pitcher Mark Langston, a fellow rookie, led the AL in strikeouts. Injuries plagued the Mariners in 1985 and 1986. Fan attendance waned as the team continued to post losing records.

A new optimism took hold in 1987. The Mariners produced a franchise-record 78 wins. Langston won 19 games. Speedy second baseman Harold Reynolds stole a team-record 60 bases. They were both All-Stars.

The following year, strapping right fielder Jay Buhner came to Seattle. Buhner knew the Mariners had work to do. "The Kingdome was so empty," he recalled, "you could hear the crickets chirping from the upper decks." The team won only 68 games.

EMERGING FROM THE DEPTHS

In 1989, the Mariners welcomed 19-year-old rookie center fielder Ken Griffey Jr. Fans called him "Junior." The young star displayed brilliant defensive skills and effortless speed. He was a power hitter, too. "I don't think anybody has ever been that good at that age," said Mariners batting coach Gene Clines. "He's in his own category."

Langston was traded early in the season. The team got towering pitcher Randy Johnson in return. Standing 6-foot-10, he was nicknamed "The Big Unit." He was inexperienced, but learned quickly. He recorded the franchise's first no-hitter on June 2, 1990. That was the start of great things.

EXTRA INNINGS

NEW YORK YANKEES VS.
SEATTLE MARINERS
AMERICAN LEAGUE DIVISION SERIES (ALDS)
OCTOBER 3–8, 1995

DOUBLE TROUBLE

It was Seattle's first postseason appearance. New York won the first two games. Seattle won the next two. The decisive Game 5 went into extra innings. New York pushed across a run in the top of the 11th. They led 5–4. Seattle second baseman Joey Cora led off the bottom of the inning with a bunt single. Griffey's single into center field sent Cora to third. Powerful designated hitter Edgar Martinez strode to the plate. He smoked a line drive down the left-field line. Cora scored easily. Griffey sprinted around second base before the ball even hit the outfield wall. He slid across home plate just ahead of the throw. The Mariners won the game, 6–5! That set off a joyful explosion on the field and in the stands. Martinez's clutch two-bagger is still known as "The Double." Dave Niehaus, the Mariners' play-by-play announcer, said, "That was the biggest hit in Mariners history!"

EXTRA INNINGS

JAY BUHNER
RIGHT FIELDER
MARINERS SEASONS: 1988–2001
HEIGHT: 6-FOOT-3
WEIGHT: 220 POUNDS
KEY STATS: .255 BATTING AVERAGE, 307 HOME RUNS, 965 RBIS, 1X ALL-STAR

BAD TO THE BONE

Many people feel that the best trade in Mariners history was sending first baseman Dick Phelps to the New York Yankees for right fielder Jay Buhner. It was even mentioned in an episode of the popular 1990s sitcom Seinfeld. With his gleaming bald head and goatee, "Bone" soon became a fan favorite. The right field stands became known as the "Boneyard." Starting in the 1990s, he presided over "Buhner Buzz Cut Night." Willing fans had their heads shaved for free admission. On June 23, 1993, Buhner became the first Mariner to hit for the cycle: a single, double, triple, and home run in the same game. Fittingly, he scored the winning run. He still ranks third in Mariners career home runs and RBIs.

Johnson posted a 130–74 record in Seattle. Edgar Martinez took over at third base. He combined slugging power with a keen batting eye. He regularly hit above .300.

Seattle's rising tide of good fortune continued. The Mariners enjoyed a winning record for the first time in 1991. They finished 83–79. "We're not losers anymore!" Davis yelled after victory number 81. "It was like we'd won the World Series," Niehaus noted.

Despite a poor performance in 1992, expectations rose. Fiery Lou Piniella took over as manager the following season. He had guided the Cincinnati Reds to a World Series title three years earlier. Fans hoped he would bring the same magic to Seattle. But a winning 1993 season was followed by another losing one.

In July 1994, several large Kingdome ceiling tiles crashed to the ground. It happened just before a game was scheduled to begin. The Mariners had to play 20 away games in 21 days. Seattle officials began discussing a proposal for a new outdoor stadium.

The stage was set for the magical 1995 season. The Mariners topped the AL West for the first time. Johnson won the Cy Young Award. Piniella was Manager of the Year. After the ALDS win over the Yankees, baseball hysteria in Seattle reached a fever pitch during the American League Championship Series (ALCS). The team won two of the first three games against the Cleveland Indians. The excitement quickly faded, though. The Indians took the next three games to win the series.

In 1996, extraordinary shortstop Álex Rodríguez played his first full season. "A-Rod" had a powerful arm and an explosive bat. He hit a major-league-leading .358 with 36 home runs. The Mariners won a team-record 85 games. They missed the Wild Card by three games.

Seattle improved to 90–72 in 1997. Johnson notched a 20–4 record. He tallied 291 strikeouts. Veteran Jamie Moyer added 17 wins. He had come to

Pitcher Jamie Moyer

the Mariners late the previous season after winning just 66 games in nine seasons with five teams. Seattle rejuvenated his career. He relied on pinpoint control rather than fastballs. He ranks second in career wins with 145. Mariner batters clobbered a franchise-record 264 home runs. Seattle topped the AL West again. But they fell to the Baltimore Orioles in the first round of the playoffs. The next season was disappointing. Johnson left midseason. The team finished 76–85.

A SEASON FOR THE AGES

Safeco Field (T-Mobile Park since 2018) opened in 1999 as an outdoor venue with a retractable roof. Seattle fans were heartbroken when Griffey departed after the season. But new center fielder Mike Cameron wowed them in 2000. He displayed incredible glove work and solid hitting. Other newcomers included pitcher Freddy García and closer Kazuhiro Sasaki. This relatively unknown crew finished a franchise-best 91–71. Seattle swept the Chicago White Sox in the ALDS. The M's pushed the Yankees to six games in the ALCS before finally falling.

Shortstop Álex Rodríguez

EXTRA INNINGS

EDGAR MARTINEZ
DESIGNATED HITTER, THIRD BASE
MARINERS SEASONS: 1987–2004
HEIGHT: 6-FOOT-0
WEIGHT: 175 POUNDS
KEY STATS: .312 BATTING AVERAGE, 309 HOME RUNS, 1,261 RBIS, 7X ALL-STAR

LEMONS TO LEMONADE

Edgar Martinez spent several years in the minor leagues because he had difficulty getting base hits. Then it took him three more years after joining the Mariners to become the regular third baseman. He won the American League batting title in 1992 with a .343 average. In an exhibition game the following spring, he tore a hamstring muscle. Eventually the injury forced him to become the team's designated hitter. It was a perfect fit. He won his second batting title in 1995 with a .356 average. He went on to earn seven All-Star nods. Longtime baseball executive Bill Bavasi called Martinez "the greatest right-handed hitter of his generation." He won the MLB Outstanding Designated Hitter Award five times. When he retired, the award was renamed the Edgar Martinez Outstanding Designated Hitter Award to honor him.

But then Rodríguez signed MLB's largest-ever free-agent contract with the Texas Rangers. Bitter fans called him "A-Fraud" and showered the field with fake money every time the Rangers came to town. It was a staggering blow. Seattle had lost arguably MLB's best infielder, outfielder, and pitcher in fewer than three seasons.

No one could have predicted what would happen in 2001. The Mariners won 116 games. That mark tied the MLB record for wins in a season. Newcomers second baseman Bret Boone and swift right fielder Ichiro Suzuki were major contributors. Boone had a league-leading 141 RBIs. It was an AL record for second basemen. Ichiro (he quickly became known by just his first name, as fans chanted "EE-CHEE-RO" every time he came to bat) made a spectacular debut after several sensational seasons in Japan. Early in the season, he had a 23-game hitting streak. He was named Rookie of the Year and Most Valuable Player (MVP). He was just the second player to achieve that distinction. He would go on to win 10 Golden Glove awards. Four pitchers won at least 15 games. Sasaki notched 45 saves. The Mariners beat the Indians in the ALDS. They advanced to the ALCS. For the second year in a row, New York stopped Seattle. The Yankees won four of five games.

Seattle won 93 games in both 2002 and 2003. But it missed the playoffs each time. Piniella jumped ship between the two seasons. The Mariners fell to a disappointing 63–99 in 2004. Still, there were reasons to celebrate. On October 1, Ichiro broke the single-season record of 257 hits. It dated back to 1920. He finished the year with 262. "I'm not a big guy, or muscular," he said, "and hopefully kids will look at me and see that somebody with a regular body can get into the record books."

The Mariners entered the 2005 season with a pair of new sluggers. They were third baseman Adrián Beltré and first baseman Richie Sexson. But the team still finished at the bottom of the AL West. On the bright side, Seattle called up 19-year-old Venezuelan pitcher Félix Hernández in midseason.

Pitcher Félix Hernández

He was a hard-throwing right-hander. Hernández went just 4–4 that season. But he had a knack for ringing up strikeouts. "King Félix" would go on to become the team's all-time leader in wins with 169, and throw the 23rd perfect game in MLB history on August 15, 2012.

In 2007, the Mariners challenged for the AL West title. Slugging outfielder Raúl Ibañez drove in 105 runs. Relief pitcher J. J. Putz had 40 saves. Seattle finished the year with 88 wins. It fell just short of the playoffs. The team's momentum came to a halt with a disappointing 2008 season. The Mariners sank to a dreadful 61–101 record.

STORMY WEATHER

Ken Griffey Jr. returned in 2009. Griffey could still swing big. He walloped 19 homers. Infielders Russell Branyan and José López added 31 and 25 dingers respectively. "King Félix" had an AL-best 19 wins. Seattle had a 24-win improvement over the previous season. But in 2010, the Mariners slumped back to 61–101. Griffey retired.

The Mariners suffered through three more losing seasons. In 2014, they signed star second baseman Robinson Canó to a 10-year contract worth more than $200 million. He helped the team to 87 victories. It missed the postseason by a single game. Seattle came close again in 2016. Designated hitter Nelson Cruz led the way. He hit 43 homers and drove in 105 runs. But the team's 86–76 record was three games shy of the playoffs.

Seattle made another run at the postseason in 2018. It led the AL West in early June. But from that point, the Houston Astros ran away with the

Third baseman Kyle Seager

SEATTLE
15

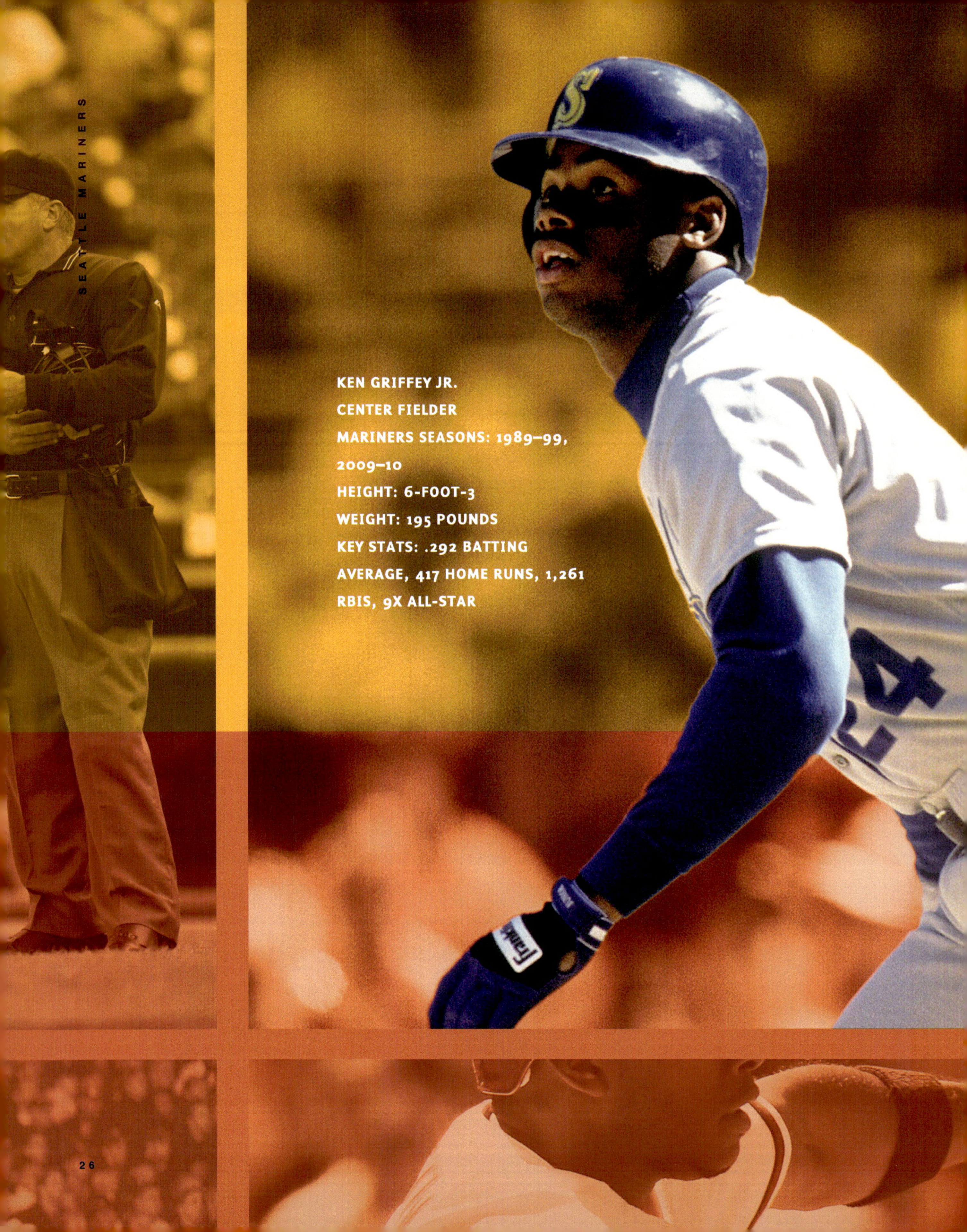

KEN GRIFFEY JR.
CENTER FIELDER
MARINERS SEASONS: 1989–99, 2009–10
HEIGHT: 6-FOOT-3
WEIGHT: 195 POUNDS
KEY STATS: .292 BATTING AVERAGE, 417 HOME RUNS, 1,261 RBIS, 9X ALL-STAR

EXTRA INNINGS

JUNIOR LEAGUE

Ken Griffey Jr.'s father was Ken Griffey Sr., a vital part of Cincinnati's Big Red Machine in the 1970s. The Mariners made Junior, as he was quickly nicknamed, the first overall pick in the 1987 MLB Draft. He hit a double in his first game with the team in 1989. He was just 19. During his decade in Seattle, he was the team's best player, hitting with power and establishing himself as one of the best center fielders in MLB. He won 10 Golden Gloves and was named AL Most Valuable Player in 1997 after hitting 56 home runs and driving in an MLB-best 147 runs. Three years later, his dad joined the M's. It was the first time that a father and son played in the same MLB game. They hit back-to-back home runs on August 14. Mariners fans were heartbroken in 1999 when Ken Jr. asked to be traded to Cincinnati to be closer to his family. He was elected to the Baseball Hall of Fame in 2016, the first year he was eligible.

division title. Seattle had to compete with Oakland for a spot in the Wild Card game. As the season wound down, Seattle cooled off and Oakland heated up. Seattle finished eight games behind the A's. Despite the late-season collapse, the 89–73 mark was sixth-best in franchise history. "Eighty-nine wins—that's hard to say it was a disappointing season," said third baseman Kyle Seager. "But at the same time, our goal was the playoffs."

Management felt that the Mariners could not compete financially with powerhouse AL teams such as Houston and New York. General manager Jerry Dipoto announced a "step-back plan." He traded most of Seattle's best players for highly-regarded prospects. Other players were released. The changes freed up the team's salary budget. Dipoto was honest with fans. He said it would take at least two years for Seattle to be competitive again.

The opening of the 2019 season astonished many people, as Seattle began 13–2. Then the expected struggles began. The Mariners developed problems in the field and at the plate. They recorded just 68 wins. Dipoto remained optimistic. "I think we've done what we said we were going to do," he said. "We identified young players, we went out and improved our farm system. . . . It's making a difference."

The Mariners were just 27–33 in the 2020 season, which was shortened due to the COVID-19 pandemic. Things were much better in 2021. Seattle posted a 90–72 mark. It was their best record since 2003. They were in a close battle for the Wild Card spots. But they fell one game short. It was the 20th year in a row of missing the postseason.

That sorry streak finally ended in 2022 with another 90–72 mark and Raleigh's dramatic home run. Julio Rodriguez was named AL Rookie of the Year. The Mariners defeated the Blue Jays in two games in the Wild Card series. But the Astros swept them in the ALDS.

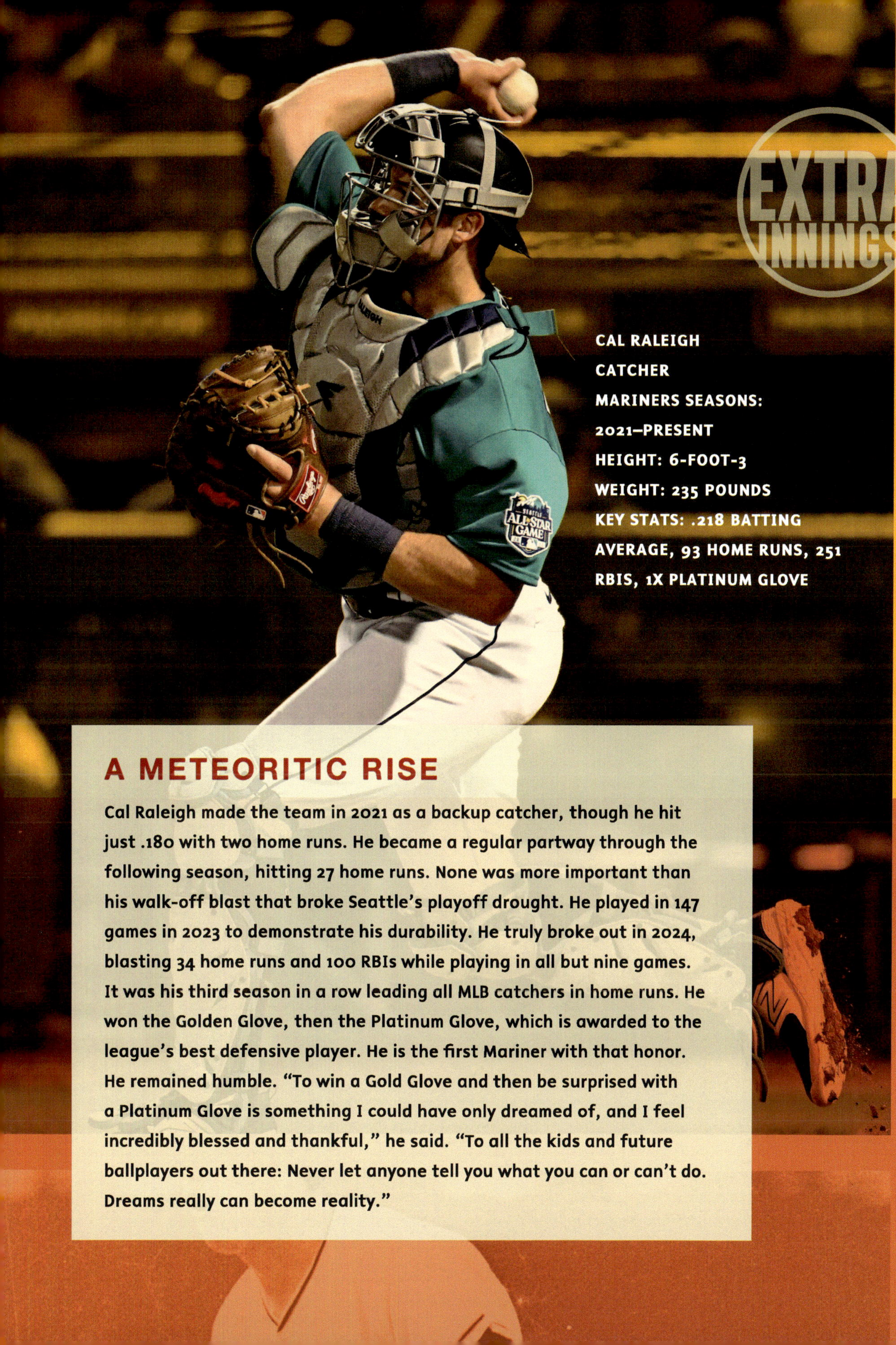

EXTRA INNINGS

CAL RALEIGH
CATCHER
MARINERS SEASONS: 2021–PRESENT
HEIGHT: 6-FOOT-3
WEIGHT: 235 POUNDS
KEY STATS: .218 BATTING AVERAGE, 93 HOME RUNS, 251 RBIS, 1X PLATINUM GLOVE

A METEORITIC RISE

Cal Raleigh made the team in 2021 as a backup catcher, though he hit just .180 with two home runs. He became a regular partway through the following season, hitting 27 home runs. None was more important than his walk-off blast that broke Seattle's playoff drought. He played in 147 games in 2023 to demonstrate his durability. He truly broke out in 2024, blasting 34 home runs and 100 RBIs while playing in all but nine games. It was his third season in a row leading all MLB catchers in home runs. He won the Golden Glove, then the Platinum Glove, which is awarded to the league's best defensive player. He is the first Mariner with that honor. He remained humble. "To win a Gold Glove and then be surprised with a Platinum Glove is something I could have only dreamed of, and I feel incredibly blessed and thankful," he said. "To all the kids and future ballplayers out there: Never let anyone tell you what you can or can't do. Dreams really can become reality."

44

Pitcher Logan Gilbert

Seattle came close to another playoff appearance in 2023, leading the AL West at the start of September. They faded and missed the playoffs by one game.

The Mariners got off to a stellar start in 2024, at one point leading the division by 10 games. They had the best five-man starting rotation in MLB. But injuries to the bullpen pitchers and a lack of hitting caused them to cool off and finish 85–77 to miss the playoffs. There was one highlight. Ichiro was voted into the Hall of Fame. He nearly became the first position player to be enshrined with a unanimous vote. One voter left Ichiro off his ballot.

In 2025, the Mariners surged to a 90–72 record, won their first AL West title since 2001, and reached the ALCS, falling in Game 7 to the Blue Jays. Cal Raleigh delivered a historic season with 60 home runs, breaking multiple MLB and franchise records. The team also retired Ichiro's number 51.

The Seattle Mariners have navigated the major-league seas for more than 40 years. They have endured choppy waters while getting occasional glimpses of the promised land. But they are the only MLB team without a World Series appearance. Fans await the day that Seattle's summertime heroes will sail to autumn baseball triumph.

Center fielder Julio Rodríguez

INDEX